Date: 6/14/12

J 636.70886 RAJ
Rajczak, Kristen.
Rescue dogs /

PALM BEACH COUNTY
LIBRARY SYSTEM
3650 SUMMIT BLVD.
WEST PALM BEACH, FL 33406

Rescue Dogs

WORKING
DOGS

By Kristen Rajczak

Gareth Stevens
Publishing

Please visit our Web site, www.garethstevens.com. For a free color catalog of all our high-quality books, call toll free 1-800-542-2595 or fax 1-877-542-2596.

Library of Congress Cataloging-in-Publication Data

Rajczak, Kristen.
Rescue dogs / Kristen Rajczak.
    p. cm. — (Working dogs)
Includes index.
ISBN 978-1-4339-4668-4 (pbk.)
ISBN 978-1-4339-4669-1 (6-pack)
ISBN 978-1-4339-4667-7 (library binding)
1. Rescue dogs. I. Title.
SF428.55.R35 2011
636.7'0886—dc22

                                    2010037169

First Edition

Published in 2011 by
Gareth Stevens Publishing
111 East 14th Street, Suite 349
New York, NY 10003

Copyright © 2011 Gareth Stevens Publishing

Designer: Michael J. Flynn
Editor: Kristen Rajczak

Photo credits: Cover, pp. 1, 9, 10, 13, 18, 20 iStockphoto.com; pp. 5, 6, 14, 17 Shutterstock.com.

All rights reserved. No part of this book may be reproduced in any form without permission in writing from the publisher, except by a reviewer.

Printed in the United States of America

CPSIA compliance information: Batch #CW11GS: For further information contact Gareth Stevens, New York, New York at 1-800-542-2595.

Contents

Words in the glossary appear in **bold** type the first time they are used in the text.

What Is a Rescue Dog?

A rescue dog helps find missing people who might be hurt. Dogs search for people in water, on land, and under snow or **rubble**. Often, dogs can find **victims** faster than search-and-rescue workers. They use their sense of smell.

Some rescue dogs work in **dangerous** places. They are trained to be calm and keep their attention on their job. These dogs like to find what they are looking for.

This rescue dog was trained to be careful when searching in rubble.

Dog Tales

In the best conditions, dogs can pick up a scent up to a half mile (0.8 km) away!

Rescue dogs may wear vests so everyone knows they are on duty.

Why Use Dogs for Rescue?

Dogs have features that make them good helpers for search-and-rescue workers. A dog's sense of smell is much stronger than a person's. A dog can track someone for miles if it knows what the person smells like. Dogs also have very good hearing and are able to see well at night. Rescue dogs can go places people cannot. They can move quickly and carefully over rocky ground, through rubble, and into small spaces.

Training

Many dogs begin training as rescue dogs when they are puppies. Training takes 1 to 2 years. Rescue dogs learn to obey and how to search for a person in many different settings. They continue to train even after they start working.

A rescue dog lives with its **handler**. Handlers may be firefighters or **volunteer** search-and-rescue workers. Rescue dogs and handlers work together. A dog lets its handler know when it finds a clue.

This rescue dog is sniffing a backpack to pick up a scent.

9

Dog Tales

When a dog picks up someone's scent, it is actually smelling skin cells that have fallen off the person.

A handler may control a rescue dog with a leash.

Air-Scent and Tracking Dogs

Air-scent dogs search for people by sniffing the air. They do not search for a single person's scent. They are trained to find any human scent and follow it. These dogs work best in wide-open spaces with few people.

Tracking dogs sniff close to the ground. They smell the clothing of a missing person before trying to find them. Then, the dog knows what scent to follow. These dogs must be used soon after the person has been in the area, so the scent is still strong.

Scent Hounds

Bloodhounds, basset hounds, and beagles are called scent hounds. They have an even better sense of smell than an average dog. These dogs are often used as tracking dogs.

Bloodhounds are black, tan, and brown with loose, wrinkled skin. They have the best sense of smell of all dogs. Basset hounds and beagles are smaller than bloodhounds. They both love to follow a scent and hunt in a group.

Dog Tales

The name "bloodhound" does not mean that these dogs sniff for blood. It means they are "blooded hounds," another name for **purebred**.

This bloodhound is using its sense of smell to help find someone.

13

Dog Tales

Rescue dogs ride in boats, trucks, and even helicopters to get to where they will search.

Snow doesn't stop a rescue dog from finding a scent. ▷

RESCUE

14

Water and Snow Search Dogs

Water search dogs help search-and-rescue workers find people missing in the water. They work on shorelines and in boats. Dogs locate the person's scent as it rises from the water. Divers then search that area.

Snow search dogs look for people trapped under the snow. The people may be skiers that were caught in an **avalanche** or someone who slipped and fell into deep snow. These dogs can smell people through as much as 15 feet (4.6 m) of snow!

Disaster Search Dogs

When a bad storm happens, buildings and homes can be destroyed. **Disaster** search dogs find victims in the rubble of broken buildings. They can smell someone buried under soil or stones. Rescue dogs helped find people after an earthquake in Haiti in 2010. They also worked on the Gulf Coast after Hurricane Katrina hit in 2005. Dogs that work in disaster areas are brave and skilled searchers. They help search-and-rescue workers find many **survivors**.

Dog Tales

Rescue dogs and their handlers came from all over the world to help the people of Haiti. They came from as far away as France and China.

It's important for hardworking disaster dogs to drink water, especially when it's hot outside.

17

German shepherds like this one learn quickly to obey their handlers.

Many Rescue Breeds

Many of the best search-and-rescue **breeds** are dogs that have worked with people throughout history. German shepherds have been used as search dogs for many years. They also are used in police and military work. They are usually black and tan, and weigh between 75 and 95 pounds (34 and 43 kg).

Newfoundlands are used in water rescue. These dogs are strong swimmers. They even have **webbed** toes! Other common rescue dog breeds are border collies and giant schnauzers.

Good Rescuers

Rescue dogs have very important jobs. With their help, many missing people are rescued and returned to their families.

There are many search-and-rescue groups in the United States that use dogs. Some of these groups include the National Association for Search and Rescue, Search and Rescue Dogs of the United States, and the American Rescue Dog Association. Dogs from these groups have helped rescue people all over the country.

SEARCH

Search-and-Rescue Dogs

Type of Dog	How It Searches
air-scent dog	sniffs the air for any human scent and follows it
tracking dog	smells an article belonging to someone and tracks that scent on the ground
water search dog	finds a person's scent in the water and leads rescuers to it
snow search dog	locates people buried under snow by finding their scent
disaster search dog	sniffs around disaster areas to find trapped people

Glossary

avalanche: a large mass of snow sliding down a mountain or over a cliff

breed: a group of animals that share features different from other groups of the kind

dangerous: unsafe

disaster: an event that causes suffering or loss

handler: a person who trains and controls an animal

purebred: an animal that has family members of only one breed

rubble: what is left of a building that has fallen

survivor: someone who lives through a disaster

victim: a person who has been hurt

volunteer: working without being paid

webbed: joined by skin

For More Information

Books:

Jackson, Donna M. *Hero Dogs: Courageous Canines in Action*. New York, NY: Little, Brown, and Company, 2003.

Presnall, Judith Janda. *Rescue Dogs*. San Diego, CA: Kidhaven Press, 2003.

Web Sites:

FBI Working Dogs: Search and Rescue Dogs
www.fbi.gov/kids/dogs/search.htm
Find out how search-and-rescue dogs work with the FBI.

Hunter's Search Dog Kids Area
www.jcsda.com/kids/
Learn more about search-and-rescue dogs.

Publisher's note to educators and parents: Our editors have carefully reviewed these Web sites to ensure that they are suitable for students. Many Web sites change frequently, however, and we cannot guarantee that a site's future contents will continue to meet our high standards of quality and educational value. Be advised that students should be closely supervised whenever they access the Internet.

Index